US COAST GUARD
Alphabet Book

UNITED STATES COAST GUARD
E PLURIBUS UNUM
SEMPER PARATUS
1790

JERRY PALLOTTA ★ **SAMMIE GARNETT** ★ Illustrated by **VICKIE FRASER**

Charlesbridge

To Josh Miller, the coolest coast guard helicopter pilot in the galaxy—J. P.

Many thanks to Brett Mastronardi and Robert Woodward for serving and deploying to both littoral and blue-water regions of the world—S. G.

To all past, present, and future coast guard members—V. F.

Published by Charlesbridge
9 Galen Street, Watertown, MA 02472
(617) 926-0329 • www.charlesbridge.com

Printed in China
(hc) 10 9 8 7 6 5 4 3 2 1

Illustrations done in mixed media
Display type set in Rockwell by Monotype
Text type set in Memphis by Adobe Systems Inc.
Printed by 1010 Printing International Limited in Huizhou, Guangdong, China
Production supervision by Jennifer Most Delaney
Designed by Cathleen Schaad and Ellie Erhart

Library of Congress Cataloging-in-Publication Data
Names: Pallotta, Jerry, author. | Garnett, Sammie, author. | Fraser, Vickie, illustrator.
Title: US Coast Guard alphabet book / Jerry Pallotta and Sammie Garnett; illustrated by Vickie Fraser.
Other titles: United States Coast Guard alphabet book
Description: Watertown, MA: Charlesbridge, [2023] | Audience: Ages 4–7 years | Audience: Grades K–1 | Summary: "This alphabet book has something about the US Coast Guard for every letter." —Provided by publisher.
Identifiers: LCCN 2022032028 (print) | LCCN 2022032029 (ebook) | ISBN 9781570919541 (hardcover) | ISBN 9781632897572 (ebook)
Subjects: LCSH: United States. Coast Guard—Juvenile literature. | Alphabet books—Juvenile literature. | English language—Alphabet—Juvenile literature.
Classification: LCC VG53 .P35 2023 (print) | LCC VG53 (ebook) | DDC 363.28/60973—dc23/eng/20220907
LC record available at https://lccn.loc.gov/2022032028
LC ebook record available at https://lccn.loc.gov/2022032029

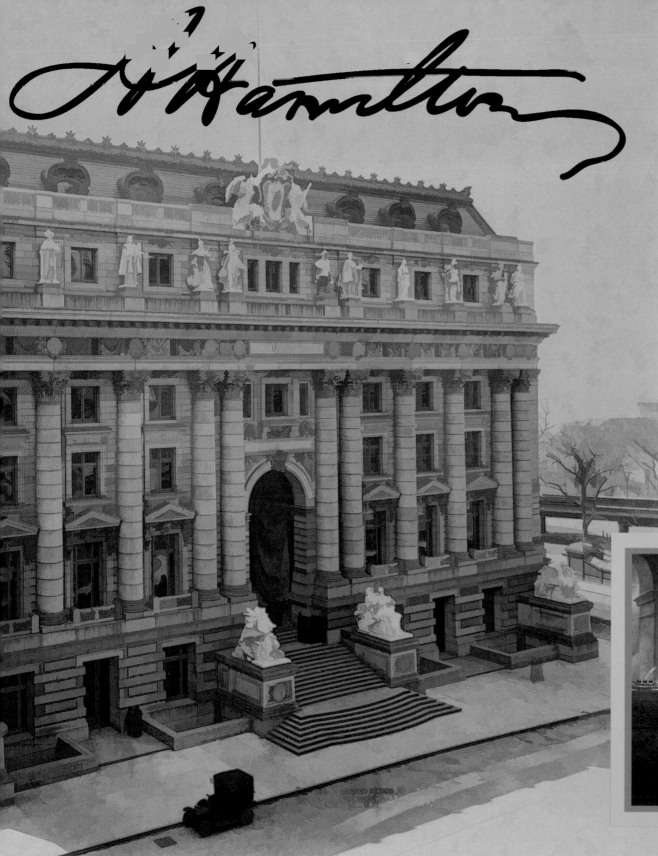

Aa

A is for Alexander Hamilton.

Treasury Secretary Alexander Hamilton wrote that our new nation needed a customs service to collect taxes from cargo-carrying ships. To collect these taxes he said the United States needed "guard boats." So the United States Coast Guard was born in 1790!

Bb

B is for Buoy. On roads we have signs. On the water the coast guard places buoys—floating canisters with colors and numbers. These markings tell ships how to navigate, or find their way safely into and out of ports. Red and green buoys show ships and boats the way. There is a helpful way to remember a navigation rule: "Red, Right, Returning." This means keep **red** buoys on the **right** side of your vessel when you're **returning** to the harbor.

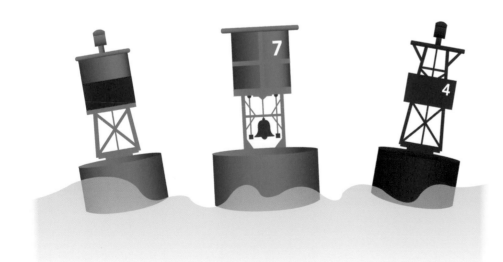

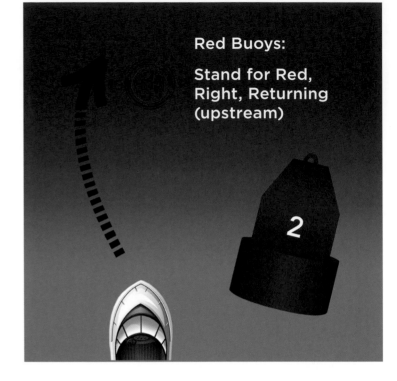

Red Buoys:

Stand for Red, Right, Returning (upstream)

Green Buoys:

Should always be kept on the port side (left) of the boat (downstream)

C is for Cutter. Cutter was the name for Alexander Hamilton's coast guard boats. Cutters were fast ships that could catch smugglers—sailors trying to sneak their ships into port without paying taxes. Today coast guard cutters are large enough to save people in any weather, yet fast enough to catch smugglers or fight pirates. Yes, there are modern pirates!

Cc

Dd

D is for Diver. Coast guard divers tend piers and buoys to ensure no harm can be done to the hull of a ship in port. To qualify to be a coast guard diver, you must be able to

- swim 500 yards (five football fields!) in 14 minutes, rest 10 minutes, and then . . .
- do 42 push-ups in 2 minutes, rest 2 minutes, and then . . .
- do 50 sit-ups in 2 minutes, rest 2 minutes, and then . . .
- do 6 pull-ups, rest 10 minutes, and then . . .
- run 1.5 miles in under 12 minutes and 45 seconds!

Wow! Do you think you could do that?

U.S. COAST GUARD

SCUBA DIVER

E is for USCGC *Eagle*. This famous sailing barque, or bark, was built in Germany prior to World War II to train naval cadets. She became an American ship after the war and was renamed *Eagle*. A barque is a beautiful sailing ship with three or more towering masts, miles of rigging, or ropes, and flowing white sails. Today *Eagle* is used to train US Coast Guard cadets.

Ee

Ff

F is for Fast Response Boat (FRB). This rescue boat is painted bright orange so everyone knows it's the coast guard. These fast boats can speed up to 40 knots per hour,

as fast as a car on a highway. FRBs are built of
strong aluminum. They can hit a submerged rock
without sinking.

IDA LEWIS
THE GRACE DARLING OF AMERICA
KEEPER OF LIME ROCK LIGHTHOUSE
NEWPORT HARBOR
BORN FEB 25 1842
DIED OCT 24 1911

ERECTED BY HER MANY KIND
FRIENDS

Gg

G is for Gold Lifesaving Medal. Civilians can earn this prestigious medal for "extreme and heroic daring" when coming to the aid of people in danger at sea. The first woman to be awarded the gold medal was Ida Lewis from Newport, Rhode Island, who made multiple trips in small boats to save stranded sailors. She is honored today with a sailing club in Newport named after her.

Hh

H is for Helicopter. The US Coast Guard has a fleet of low-flying helicopters that can be used to find lost ships at sea. A coast guard helicopter can hover above a disabled ship, lower a rescue basket, and save stranded crew members.

Ii

I is for Icebreaker. US Coast Guard icebreakers are large, thick-hulled ships that can push through frozen ocean channels. This allows merchant ships to continue their voyage safely.

J is for Jacob's Ladder. Originally Jacob's ladder was a biblical reference for climbing to heaven. In mariner's language, it is a ladder lowered over the side of a ship to rescue sailors. In 1952, the shipwrecked crew of the *Pendleton* threw their Jacob's ladder over the side of their stranded ship. One by one the sailors carefully climbed down the ladder to a waiting coast guard ship that was sent to rescue them.

Kk

K is for Knot. A knot can tie together two ropes on a ship. Ropes are used to tie ships to docks, raise flags up masts, and secure cargo. But "knot" also has another meaning: speed. In the sailing age (before 1850), sailors put a weight on the end of a long rope with knots tied in spaced intervals. A crew member threw the rope over the side of the ship at the bow (the front) and counted how much time it took it to reach the stern (the back). This measured the ship's speed through the water. For example, five lengths of knots meant five knots of speed (about 10 miles per hour.) Today we still use knots to describe the speed of boats and ships.

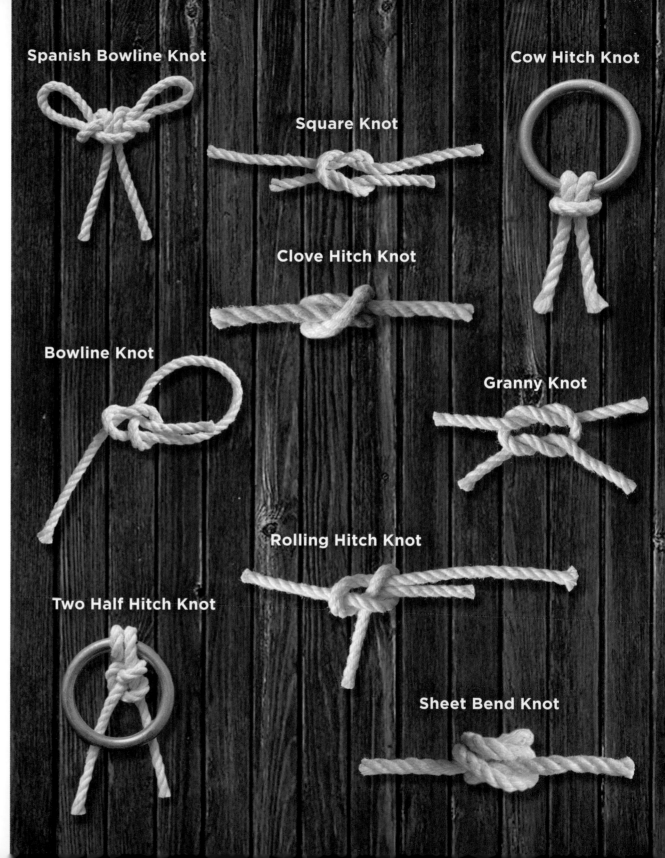

Spanish Bowline Knot

Square Knot

Cow Hitch Knot

Clove Hitch Knot

Bowline Knot

Granny Knot

Rolling Hitch Knot

Two Half Hitch Knot

Sheet Bend Knot

L is for Lightship. Lightships were first used in England in 1732 to mark dangerous shoals in places where lighthouses could not be built. In 1820, the United States began using lightships along the coast, usually moored near rocky or shallow waters, warning ships to keep clear. Most lightships are now retired, replaced by automated buoys that don't need a human to operate them. A few original Nantucket lightships have survived, two of which are in Boston Harbor. A third sister ship is moored in New Bedford, Massachusetts.

Ll

Mm

M is for Mayday. When a ship is in danger and must call the coast guard for help, it sends out a "mayday" emergency call. The term *mayday* originated from the French phrase *m'aider*, which means "Help me!"

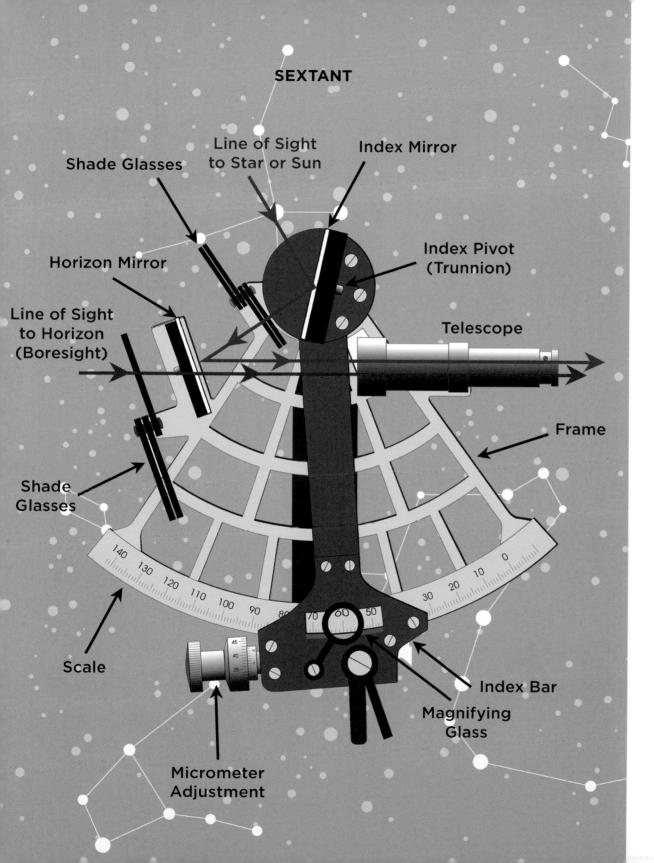

SEXTANT

Shade Glasses

Line of Sight to Star or Sun

Index Mirror

Horizon Mirror

Index Pivot (Trunnion)

Line of Sight to Horizon (Boresight)

Telescope

Frame

Shade Glasses

140 130 120 110 100 90 80 70 60 50 30 20 10 0

45 40 35

Scale

Index Bar

Magnifying Glass

Micrometer Adjustment

Nn

N is for Navigation.
Thousands of years ago, the Egyptians, Romans, and Chinese navigated their ships by observing the stars. Today the coast guard teaches cadets navigation using some of the same old tools, such as a sextant and a star chart. Today most ships and recreational boats have computers with powerful satellite-based navigation systems (also called GPS or Global Positioning System). Even smartphones can be used to navigate if the power ever goes out!

Oo

O is for Operations Center. The US Coast Guard has large offices in many coastal cities to monitor shipping traffic and emergency calls. Officers watch large computer screens that show all the ships nearby. They're also ready to assist a faraway ship that calls for help, sending its location via longitude and latitude. With this crucial information, an operations center can send helicopters or ships to rescue a stranded ship or boat.

Coast Guard Operations Center

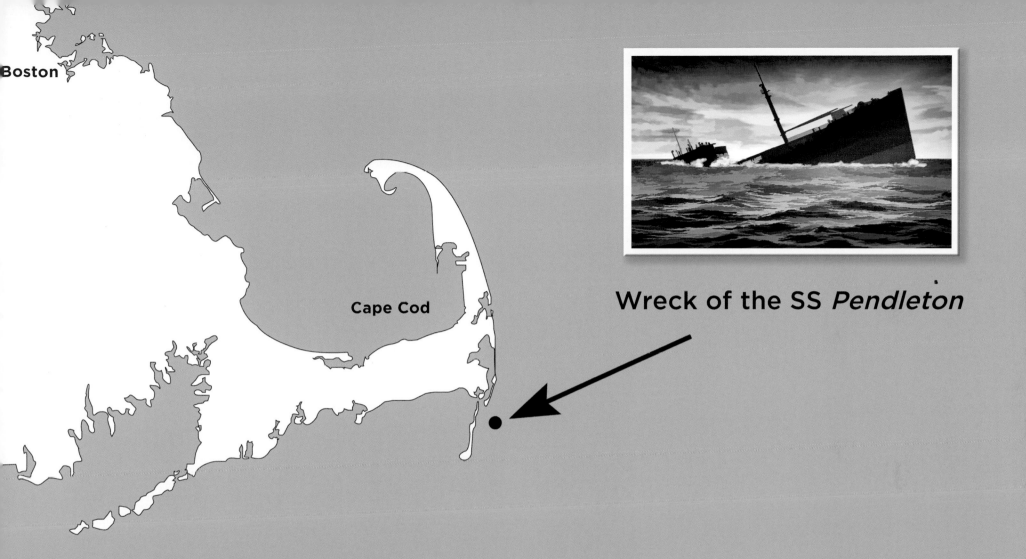

Boston

Cape Cod

Wreck of the SS *Pendleton*

P is for *Pendleton*. This was one of the most famous sea rescues of all time! In 1952, a large tanker ship named *Pendleton* was wrecked in a storm off the coast of Cape Cod, Massachusetts. The big ship broke into two pieces. The coast guard left Chatham in the middle of the night, braving huge waves, cold winds, ice, and snow to rescue the crew. Sadly not every sailor on the *Pendleton* could be found. But the coast guard rescued as many survivors as possible and found its way back to harbor in the stormy night.

Pp

Qq

Q is for Quarantine. Quarantine is a strategy the coast guard uses to isolate a ship with people aboard who have infectious illnesses. This helps stop the spread of diseases. The yellow Q signal flag designates a ship under quarantine. Q could also stand for "Queen of the Fleet," the nickname of the oldest commissioned coast guard cutter.

Rr

R is for Revenue Cutter Service. Remember how Alexander Hamilton founded the coast guard when America was still a new country? It needed to collect taxes on goods sold into the United States. So the Revenue Cutter Service was formed, and guard ships ensured that all cargo ships paid their duties before coming ashore. Today we have an established tax system, so we don't need these ships anymore.

Ss

S is for Ship. Question: What is a simple difference between a ship and a boat? Answer: A boat can fit onto a ship! But a ship can't fit onto a boat! The US Coast Guard operates ships, such as cutters, and boats, such as FRBs. Do some research. Which of these vessels are ships and which are boats?

Barque

Longboat

Buoy Tender

Patrol Boat

Cutter

Rigid Inflatable Boat (RIB)

Icebreaker

Tt

T is for Transom. Transom is another word for the back of a ship or a boat. If you are floating in the water hoping to be rescued, you don't want to see a ship's transom. You'd have to yell, "Please, come back!" When boating, always wear a PFD (personal flotation device), which should be a coast guard approved life jacket.

Transom
Height

Transom
Width

U is for Uniforms. There are many different uniforms in the US Coast Guard. Unlike our other armed services—army, navy, marines, and air force—the coast guard does not report to the US Defense Department. After the September 11, 2001, attack on our country, the coast guard became part of the Department of Homeland Security. We are fortunate to have men and women dedicated to helping keep us safe at sea. The next time you see a coast guard ship or boat in a harbor near you, wave and thank them for their service!

Uu

Vv

V is for *Vineyard* Lightship Wreck. In 1944, during World War II, a ferocious hurricane struck the East Coast of the United States. Lightships were "on station," anchored near treacherous rocky waters or shallows. The *Vineyard* was caught in this terrible storm near Martha's Vineyard. Seven crewmen on board couldn't return to the harbor in time. Its anchor cables split, and the ship drifted away. While its location was determined nine days later, it wasn't until 1963 that explorers really investigated her wreckage. Today those seven brave lightship sailors are honored on a plaque in New Bedford, Massachusetts.

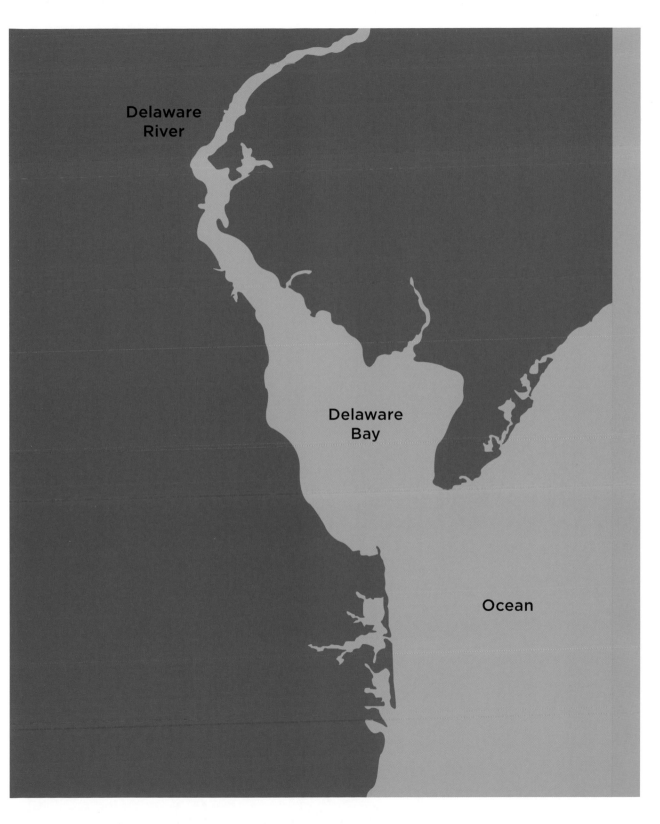

Delaware
River

Delaware
Bay

Ocean

W is for Waterways. Where can you find the coast guard? In waterways, bodies of water through which ships or boats navigate. Waterways include oceans, rivers, lakes, gulfs, bays, canals, estuaries, and more.

Xx

X is for Executive Officer.

An executive officer, known as an XO, is a ship's second-in-command officer. Other coast guard officers include commanding officer, operations specialist, and engineer officer.

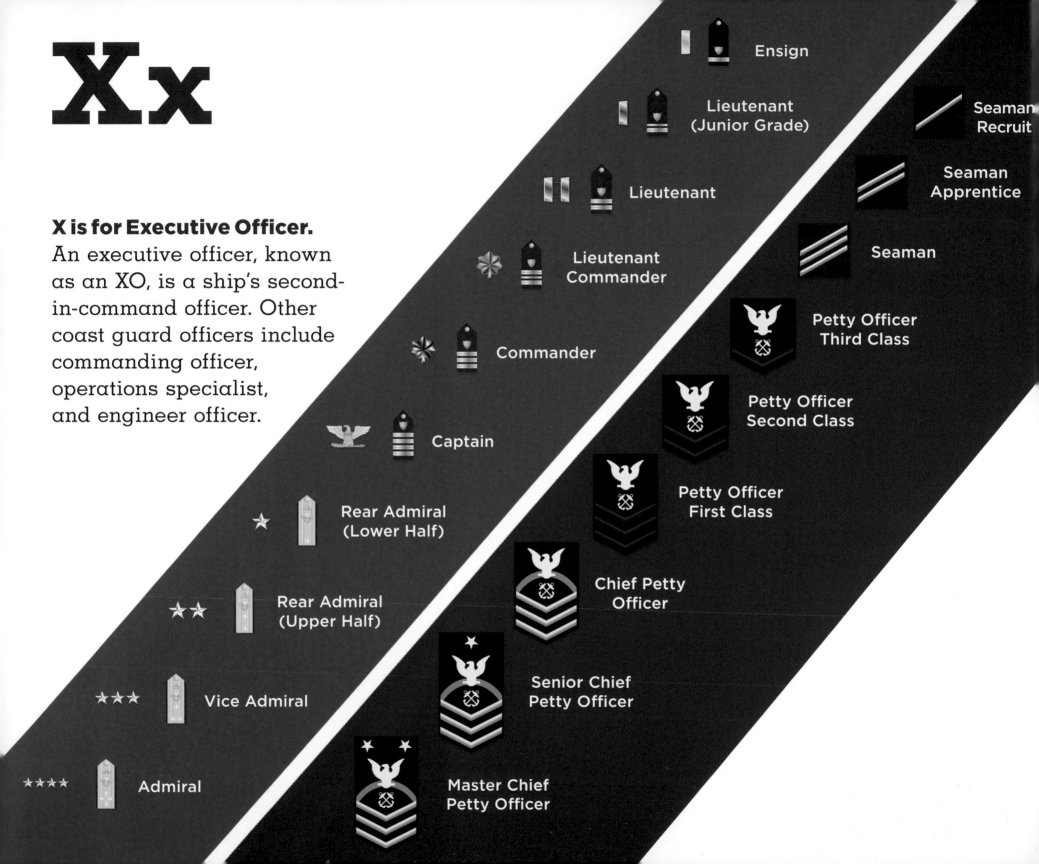

Ensign

Lieutenant (Junior Grade)

Lieutenant

Lieutenant Commander

Commander

Captain

Rear Admiral (Lower Half)

Rear Admiral (Upper Half)

Vice Admiral

Admiral

Seaman Recruit

Seaman Apprentice

Seaman

Petty Officer Third Class

Petty Officer Second Class

Petty Officer First Class

Chief Petty Officer

Senior Chief Petty Officer

Master Chief Petty Officer

Y is for Yardarm. A yardarm is where sailing ships, such as the *Eagle*, hang their sails. It is a crossbar attached to the mast. Yardarms are also attached to coast guard flagpoles to honor the coast guard's heritage and history.

Zz

Z is for Zenith. A zenith is the highest point in the sky directly above a ship. Sailors once used the zenith to help navigate their ships or boats.

Fun quiz:

Question: If you make a mathematical error while navigating, is that a big problem?

Answer: Yes, unless you want to steer your ship into a cliff!

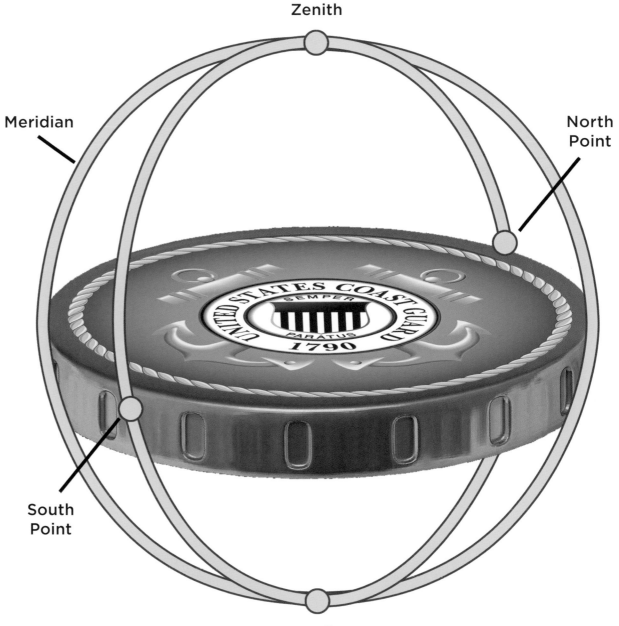

Zenith

Meridian

North Point

South Point

Nadir

MORE ABOUT THE COAST GUARD

The US Coast Guard has had many roles over the years. Today it protects our shores from any enemy or criminal, and does the important work of search and rescue. It also helps to protect and preserve sea life. It is the smallest branch of the armed forces with just over 50,000 active duty members who protect 95,000 miles of coastline. We are very fortunate to have men and women dedicated to helping keep us safe.

On an average day, the coast guard does the following:
- conducts 45 search and rescue cases
- saves 10 lives
- conducts 57 waterborne patrols of maritime infrastructure
- escorts 5 high-capacity passenger vessels
- screens 360 merchant vessels prior to arrival in ports
- services 82 buoys and aids to navigation
- investigates 35 pollution incidents
- conducts 105 marine inspections
- facilitates movement of $8.7 billion worth of goods through the nation's Maritime Transportation System

This list is adapted from an article by Lt. Sarah Janaro, "A Day in the Life of the Coast Guard: Monday," *The Maritime Executive*, March 7, 2017.

SEMPER PARATUS!

"Always Ready" is the motto of the US Coast Guard.